SHIRLEY GREENWAY

ANIMAL HOMES

BURROWS

photographs by Oxford Scientific Films

Newington Press

First published in the
United States in 1991 by
Newington Press
2 Old New Milford Road
Brookfield, Connecticut 06804

First published in Great Britain
in 1990 by Belitha Press Limited

Library of Congress Cataloging-in-Publication Data
Greenway, Shirley
Animal homes: burrows/Shirley Greenway;
photographs by Oxford Scientific Films.
Brookfield, Conn.: Newington Press, 1991.
24 p.: col. ill.; 21 cm (Animal homes)
Explains how the kingfisher, swallow, mole,
badger, rabbit, red fox, and trapdoor spider live
in burrows and care for their young.
1. Burrowing animals—Juvenile literature.
2. Animals—Habitations—Juvenile literature
I. Oxford Scientific Films. II. Title. III. Series.
ISBN: 1-878137-11-5   591.564

Words in **bold** are explained in the glossary at the
end of this book.

Burrows make good homes. They are cool resting places when it's hot and dry, and warm when it's cold and wet. Above all, burrows are safe places to raise young animals away from the danger of **predators**.

A pair of kingfishers (left and above) have built their nest in a steep-sided riverbank where the fishing is good. Both parents dig the nest tunnel and fish to feed the newly hatched young. Kingfishers are expert fishers. They can catch more than one hundred fish in a day.

Most members of the large swallow family like to nest in separate pairs, carefully defending their own small **territory**. But bank swallows are more neighborly. A hardworking pair will spend several days patiently digging a tunnel 3 feet (1 meter) long in a steep riverbank. Then they settle into a tidy burrow in a noisy high-rise tenement—along with hundreds of other pairs of nesting bank swallows.

Here they lay their eggs. The parents take turns, one sitting on the nest to **incubate** the eggs while the other hunts for insects. When the eggs hatch, the hunting becomes more intense. Each parent returns to the burrow every few minutes with a beakful of juicy flies. By the time the nestlings are ready to hunt for themselves, their exhausted parents will have fed them almost 200,000 insects!

5

Its **medieval** name was *moldewarp*—or earth thrower— and the little black mole is one of nature's best known burrowers. This silky-coated little creature is solidly built for pushing its way through the loose earth as it digs swiftly with large, strong claws. The hardworking mole can shift twice its own weight in earth every minute—and eats half its weight in earthworms every day to keep up its strength. As the mole digs, the soft soil is pushed aside and sometimes up to the surface to form the earthy mound we call a molehill.

6

A mole may build 660 feet (200 meters) of tunnels leading out from the round, grassy nest in which the young are cared for—well protected in their underground home. The usually solitary moles mate in February, and the tiny hairless babies are born in April or May. For the next month the female looks after them—scampering quickly along the tunnels searching for earthworms as they drop from the walls. She can run swiftly underground—forward *and* backward—with the help of sensitive whiskers on her nose and tail.

With its long, silky coat and distinctively striped head, the badger is one of the most easily recognized woodland animals—if you are lucky enough to see one, that is. For this powerful animal is also **nocturnal** and shy, coming out of its underground burrow only during the hours of darkness. Badgers will move quickly if disturbed during their nighttime rambles in search of food. Small **mammals**, worms, and snails are among a badger's favorite foods, but it will eat almost *anything*.

Each badger clan has its own stoutly defended **territory**, where a group of badgers lives together in a large rambling

burrow called a sett. The adults of each clan are tireless burrowers, constantly repairing and extending the chambers and tunnels of their home sett. Their daytime sleeping nests are lined with hay for extra comfort, as the badgers spend a great deal of time at home in their setts.

Badgers choose a mate for life, and the parents raise their cubs together. The young remain underground for almost two months before going out to follow the adults on their nightly hunting expeditions. The careful badger parents keep their cubs close by until they are six months old and well able to look after themselves.

9

Rabbits are the best known of all burrowing animals. They build large complex burrows called warrens. The burrows are linked by a series of tunnels, forming an underground city that is the home of a whole **colony** of rabbits. They spend the day underground and come out at dusk to feed. Keeping close to a handy bolt hole, the rabbits **graze** through the night over familiar territory, its edges marked with shallow scrapes or piles of droppings. If any danger comes, one rabbit will warn the others by thumping hard with its hind foot. The rabbits all scamper back to the safety of their burrows.

In the spring female rabbits, or **does**, dig burrows a little way from the warren. They are shallow and snug and lined with leaves and fur. When their babies are born, the does close the entrances to their nesting burrows and return to the main **colony**. For the next three weeks they will slip away every night to feed their young. When they are old enough to venture out to feed, the young rabbits follow their mothers as they **graze**. Rabbits have enormous families—each doe can have as many as thirty young every year.

Red fox cubs are born deep underground, on the bare floor of a warm, dry den, called an earth. Tree roots make a strong, safe roof over the earth, and long tunnels lead to its secret entrances.

At first the **vixen** cares for her little blind newborn cubs by herself, but it can be a tough job. When she is ready to hunt again, other vixens—aunts and sisters of the cubs— help her to look after the newborn cubs. As the cubs grow stronger and more curious, these "baby-sitters" play a greater part in their lives—grooming them, feeding them, and teaching them the hunting skills and ways of an adult.

The springhare seems to have been created from parts of many different animals—with its foxy red tail, long rabbit ears, big brown mouse's eyes, tiny front paws, and the strong back legs of a kangaroo. But it all adds up to a very successful animal. In spite of being the favorite food of many meat eaters, the springhare thrives in the dry grasslands of southern Africa.

Their body design also makes springhares highly efficient burrowers. They close their eyes, flatten their ears, and dig rapidly with long-clawed front paws, while pushing away the loosened earth with their big spade-like back feet. Each

springhare builds its own private burrow, where it spends the hot daylight hours. In the evening they leave their safe burrow homes and come out to feed, staying together for protection. Many eyes dart to catch the slightest movement and many ears twitch to hear the smallest sounds.

Females give birth several times a year to one baby at a time. For eight weeks the mother shares her cramped burrow with her large offspring—often sleeping with it cradled on her lap. The young grow fast—feet and ears first! They soon learn the swift hopping run and 9-foot (3-meter) jumps that get the little springhares safely back to their burrows.

The plains of North America are the home of the highly sociable prairie dogs. Cone-shaped mounds of earth dotted over the open ground mark the outer limits of a prairie dog "town." These well-organized **rodents** live in "neighborhoods" within each town and post sentries to warn of any approaching danger. Members of the same neighborhood greet each other by touching noses, but any stranger is warned away with a loud doglike bark.

The underground nests are connected by a network of tunnels, and a great many friendly visits take place during the warm summer months. Winter brings the cold weather and the birth of the young, and each family retreats into the cozy world of its burrow. Warm weather tempts the young out into the sunshine—to play with their parents and meet the other new citizens of the town.

The trapdoor spider is a *very* careful builder. First, it digs a long, deep hole in the ground. Then it spins a thread of silk, which it uses to line the sides of the hole with a smooth covering. Finally, the spider constructs a neat lid out of soil and silk and attaches it with a strong silken hinge. Hidden under moss and leaves, the burrow makes a safe, dry home for the large, hairy trapdoor spider.

But the spider isn't *just* making itself a comfortable home. The tightly lidded burrow also makes an excellent "hunting lodge." Lurking just below the slightly open lid, the spider waits patiently until a likely victim comes near. Then out it pops, grabs its **prey**, and disappears with amazing speed—another successful ambush!

Scorpions, too, spend their days in burrows that they dig in the sandy soil. Scorpions live in all the world's warm regions, especially the deserts. They come out to hunt at night in the cool darkness, which helps to protect them from **predators**. These large relatives of spiders have strong lobsterlike pincers on their front legs, and powerful, poisonous stings in the tips of their arched tails. They have a bad reputation, but scorpions use their stings more for protection than attack.

A scorpion mother piles her newborn babies into a tangled heap on her back and carries them with her wherever she goes. When the young are fully developed, they shed their skins for the first time. Then they are ready to leave their mother—and eat their first meal.

Some unexpected animals spend part of their complex lives underground. The beautiful spurge hawk moth of the Mediterranean begins life as a tiny egg clinging to a leaf. The egg becomes a brightly colored caterpillar. Its red, black, white, and orange body is easily seen among the leaves of the spurge—its favourite food plant.

Later the bright caterpillar wriggles into a tunnel under the earth and spins itself a silken cocoon. As this **chrysalis** forms, its hard brown shell fits snugly into its burrow. As time passes the caterpillar's body inside the chrysalis changes into a completely new creature—a fully grown spurge hawk moth.

When the cocoon splits, the adult moth struggles out from under the ground and up into the air—its final home.

Index/Glossary

badger 8–9
bank swallow 5

caterpillar 22
chrysalis a stage of an insect's life
  when it is changing into an adult 22
colony a number of animals of the
  same kind living together 10, 11

desert 21
doe a female hare, rabbit, or deer 11

fox 12

graze feed on growing plants 10, 11

incubate to keep eggs warm to hatch
  them 5

kingfisher 3

mammal a warm-blooded furry
  animal that feeds its young with its
  own milk 8
medieval the historical period known
  as the Middle Ages (from about the
  5th to the 15th centuries) 6
mole 6–7
moth 22

nocturnal of the night 8

prairie dogs 16
predator an animal that kills
  another animal for food 3, 21
prey an animal that is killed and
  eaten by another animal 19

rabbits 10–11
red fox 12
rodent a gnawing animal, such as a
  mouse or rat 16

scorpions 21
sett 8, 9
spider, trapdoor 19
springhare 14–15
spurge hawk moth 22
swallows 5

territory the area where an animal
  lives that it will defend against
  rivals 5, 8
trapdoor spider 19

vixen an adult female fox 12

warren 10–11

Photo Credits
The publishers wish to thank the following for
permission to reproduce copyright material:
Oxford Scientific Films for front cover (Tony
Allen); title page and p 16 (Animals Animals—
Zig Leszczynski); p 2 (Barry Walker); p 3 (Terry
Heathcote); p 4 (G. A. Maclean); p 5 (Mike
Birkhead); pp 6 and 7 (David Thompson); pp 8,
9, 13 and back cover (Robin Redfern); pp 10, 11
and 12 (G. I. Bernard); pp 14 and 15 (Chrissie
Houghton); p 17 (Animals Animals—David C.
Fritts); pp 18 and 21 (J. A. L. Cooke); p 19 (Mantis
Wildlife Films); p 20 (London Scientific Films); pp
22 and 23 (Raymond Blythe).